YOUR KNOWLEDGE HAS VALUE

Markus Volk

Open Linked Data, Open Government Data Sets

GRIN Publishing

Imprint:

Copyright © 2011 GRIN Verlag, Open Publishing GmbH
Print and binding: Books on Demand GmbH, Norderstedt Germany
ISBN: 978-3-640-93058-6

This book at GRIN:

http://www.grin.com/en/e-book/172981/open-linked-data-open-government-data-sets

GRIN - Your knowledge has value

Since its foundation in 1998, GRIN has specialized in publishing academic texts by students, college teachers and other academics as e-book and printed book. The website www.grin.com is an ideal platform for presenting term papers, final papers, scientific essays, dissertations and specialist books.

Visit us on the internet:

http://www.grin.com/

http://www.facebook.com/grincom

http://www.twitter.com/grin_com

Open Linked Data, Open Government Data Sets

Markus Volk

Studiengang: Informationsmanagement
Seminar: Anwendungen der Verwaltungsinformatik,
WS 2010/11

Universität Koblenz-Landau
Campus Koblenz
Institut für Wirtschafts- und Verwaltungsinformatik

ABSTRACT

Since late 2009 there has been a tendency towards a previously unknown openness in providing governmental data to the public. Valuable data sources are opened not only to selected scientists, but everybody who has internet connection available. The following shall be an overview on Open Linked Data, Government Data Sets and how they are made available in different parts of the world. Starting with the U.K. countries in northern Europe, the U.S.A and Australia have already opened up their databases to the public. The different ways and similarities in Open Data, Government Data and Linked Open Government Data shall be outlined. Furthermore the different user groups and their needs will be considered.

Categories and Subject Descriptors
H.4 [**Information Systems**]: public information systems

General Terms
Management, Documentation, Design, Economics, Standardization

Keywords
Linked Data, Open Data, Linked Open Government Data, Semantic Web, data.gov, data.gov.uk

1. INTRODUCTION

During the last few years the giant amounts of data the governments around the world hold has become more and more part of public interest. These data sets collected by governmental organizations contain valuable data for the economy, education and science.

The web has become the mayor source of information and so it was only logical that at a certain point in time parts of the governmental data would become desired to be available for more people. Together with the open source movement all over the world finally Open Data appeared.

Several years ago Project Gutenberg appeared and made available great literature of the past. The first version documents were completely without any links and mainly those were not even needed. It was aimed at users who would read ancient books that are no longer protected by copyright. In fact there are several of these isolated projects.

Now that governments all over the world feel an increasing pressure for more transparency they started opening their data to the web, too. One of the most known attempts might be the "Open government directive"[1] by the U.S. President in December 2009. The result of this directive was widely noticed and the amount of data published on the U.S. page data.gov has grown rapidly as Castro [5] summarized just four month after the directive.

On the other side of the Atlantic such efforts have been started in Great Britain, too[2]. The corresponding data.gov.uk provides a large number of data for the public. In the EU a long existing data source called Eurostat is now becoming increasingly known and demanded. Since 2003 the EU PSI Directive[3] simply demands the opening of governmental data. This directive must be implemented into national laws of European Union member states and is the driving force behind the efforts across Europe.

Furthermore, the data sources are being more and more connected by simple links and new web technologies. The increased possibilities and needs to provide not only data, but also a context leads to emerging semantic web technology. The often so called Web 3.0 develops with new technologies and standards. Different use and purposes are developing, becoming more web based and attracting different groups of users. What was only open to some scientists in the past is becoming accessible and interesting for the broad and heterogeneous web community. The existing target groups of different users addressed are changing and increasing, which results in different considerations for the ways to present and connect existing and new data.

---

1 http://www.whitehouse.gov/sites/default/files/microsites/ogi-progress-report-american-people.pdf.

2 See Chapter 5.2 for data.gov.uk and regional British projects

3 See Chapter 5.3 for details on European projects following the demands of the directive

2. Overview on the Terms

As simple as the terms sound, there are still slightly different views on what they mean. Such terms come up through the internet and develop more or less naturally, this means they are not standardized by any organization. Other terms are developed and explained by organizations like W3C.

Some of the definitions are explicitly defined in reliable sources, other are implicitly formed by the combination of well defined terms and the use of this combination.

2.1 Open Data

When is Open Data really "open"? Open Data is data available for the use by others. This data is shared in order to be used and republished. Among the different definitions "widest possible use of data" is turning up repeatedly. The use of Open Data is generally not restricted. It can be used by individuals and organizations, where commercial use is not explicitly excluded. Open Data can also be downloaded, copied and distributed by everybody. The results of this data being used can also be published.

In some cases there is still a non-commercial clause in place, but following most organizational definitions on the web, this is not really open data [4].

Following a clear definition for open data: "A piece of knowledge is open if you are free to use, reuse, and redistribute it."[4]

The model of creative common licenses[5] also provides a definition of several grades of openness under licenses from simply allowing an unchanged distribution up to allowing almost anything with just an obligation to mention the original creator. These licenses can include or exclude commercial use, forming six versions[6].

Open Data doesn't necessarily mean that this data is linked in one or the other way. Nevertheless Open Data means that it can be linked in one or the other way.

2.2 Linked data

The term Linked Data alone doesn't mean that this data is open, in the first place it is linked to other data of the same or an other kind [13]. Like there can be Open Data that is not linked, there can be Linked Data that is not fully open.

Some data might not have a meaning alone, but become useful as soon as it is linked to other data. Even meaningful data can be enriched and become more meaningful once it is linked to other data. Other data might be misleading without connection to the right context [8].

2.3 Open Linked Data

Open Linked Data is simply Open Data that has been connected with links that add value to this data.

---

4   http://www.opendefinition.org

5   http://en.wikipedia.org/wiki/Creative_Commons http://creativecommons.org/

6   The six license types "CC BY", "CC BY-ND", "CC BY-NC-SA", "CC BY-SA", "CC BY-NC", "CC BY-NC-ND" with full license contents and legal code are provided on: http://creativecommons.org/licenses/

A well known example of Open Linked Data is Wikipedia. Since such a framework of Open Linked Data is a never complete task, it can only be achieved with the participation of the enormous workforce available within the community like in the Open Data Movement. Open Linked Data doesn't necessarily follow standards, but it is desirable to follow standards to make usage easier.

Open Linked Data is one of the major stepping stones on the path to the more standardized, planned and modeled semantic web. Some sources of data are naturally desired to be usable in such open linked ways, but traditionally are not available as such. Among these large sources with increasing value through the technical development and possibility to process large data amounts is Government Data.

2.4 Government Data
Government Data is not born as Open Data. Government Data can and always will exist in non-open forms. Some Government Data must even remain confidential for security purpose, but other data can be published for the sake of transparency or its value to science and economy[7].

There is increasingly more Open Government Data these days, but nothing secures that this data is linked to other data. Some Government Data alone might be useless even if being openly available. The data might miss the context through linkage or usability for non-governmental users. There has been government data on the web for years, e. g. on Eurostat. Most of the available data was simply published without much context. The target group was small and users consisted mainly of scientists, students, politicians and some mainly large companies.

Nowadays this is changing. Governments are trying to show more transparency and publishing data sets is a rather simple way to show these efforts.

2.5 Open Government Data Sets
Just publishing Government Data is not a very interesting thing anymore. With the development of new technologies this data needs to be combined and complete data sets are desired instead of just slices of the existing data. The data sets shall not simply cover parts, but give a broader view on the issues. One of the widest known examples is the gross domestic product, which is not so interesting or scientifically useful alone, so it is usually published in relations to previous years or other countries.

Data Sets of all fields of public service can be interesting to scientists. A more challenging task is the to publish the data targeting at all possible users of the web community. Since such aims are hardly reachable the context and usability can be created by participation of the online community itself [1]. The semantic web technology provided the framework for a development towards Linked Open Government Data.

2.6 Linked Open Government Data
The term Linked Open Government Data (LOGD)[7] has been established where Open Government Data Sets are embedded in portals linking this data in the standards of the Semantic Web. LOGD includes some kind of infrastructure that supports the Open Government Data and makes it more valuable and usable.

To return to the example of the gross domestic product, it is possible to add information about price levels and relative purchasing power. The more data we link to this, the more conclusions we can draw from it.

---

7   Alternative term "Open Linked Government Data" can be found on Wikipedia and among Google Search Words

Once these data sets a properly linked very user-friendly applications can return data like consumption data for certain areas by just entering a postcode and choosing form available data sets [15].

3. Data Quality's path to Semantic Web

Open Data can be available in different forms and qualities. The data can simply be offered for downloading or embedded somehow to enrich it, or the possible use.

3.1 Raw data

Raw Data can be in diverse formats without connection to other information. This data can be simply visible or downloadable from a web page. Providing such raw data is not a new phenomenon. Raw data has been provided to non-governmental institutions through the internet long before it became a connected web like nowadays. In the early days of the internet such data was simply available for education research etc. The new issue about the raw data you can download these days is, that it is open to everybody and easily discoverable to a much greater audience.

Raw data might be there in classic formats like TXT, CSV or a bit more modern in XML or formats like Excel and other Microsoft Office formats, that are also supported by open source products. Such Raw Data can be used in several local applications or be embedded into web applications by the user. Most Raw Data is provided as tables or spreadsheets, sometimes with some explanation that will help to put it into some context.

The Raw Data might be linkable in different ways. It might only be possible to place links somewhere else that lead to the download. In that case it will remain a kind of dead end for the traffic lead there, that leaves people just to return to the origin of the link for more related information.

It might be possible that there can also be links placed to the data to make it linked data. If this is there, it is meant to become linked data, and the tasks of linking it is just left to the open source and web community in order to save public funds. Such prepared data will become linked data within very short time after the go-live of the portal.

3.2 Linked Data

Linked Data means that the data is connected to other related data in the first place. Anyway there is a difference between simple links and more related information coming with the links. The linking might happen in different ways, making it difficult to compare them. Since this has always been a problem in the web world, there have been efforts to standardize them.

The definitions of linked data have been published by on W3C.ORG by Tim Berners-Lee as "rules" and "steps"[2]:

1. *Use URIs as names for things*

2. *Use HTTP URIs so that people can look up those names*
3. *When someone looks up a URI, provide useful information (RDF, SPARQL)*
4. *Include links to other URIs, so that they can discover more things*

These steps particularly focus on a very strict format and specific path and he even demands his rules to be followed to let it be called a part of the semantic web.[8]

On the other hand Berners-Lee explicitly writes that breaking theses rules does no harm at all, but simply leaves a connection opportunity deserted. Anyway such linkage opportunities are rarely lost and just need to be taken later by changing the data in the appropriate way during the next update.

The British view published by JISC cetis is less strict and doesn't demand solely RDF or SPARQL standards. Therefore publications by JISC list the requirements a little more general and call it a powerful set of behaviors[9]:

- Named objects and resources
- Usage of web structures
- easily discoverable
- Linking (if possibility and related data known)

As different as the two sound from there wording, they lead into the same direction. A project connecting Wikipedia content to other data on the web using RDF is dbpedia.org which tries to connect web applications and e. g. geographical data. [4].

There might also be linked data that clearly doesn't respect all of the rules Berners-Lee published in 2006. If the practical needs change over time, those rules might need to be revised.

It must always be clear that these standards, rules and desired behaviors are not binding. Data that is linked in different ways or with different technology can still be linked to data that follows the rules.

For Linked Government Data there is a special challenge attached. In most countries there need to be laws or directives for everything a government does. Since the Linked Data principles are rather new, it is a great challenge to get opening data going and adapting the changing needs of a new technology. On both sides of the Atlantic there are different ideas behind the paths to open data. Rather new standards also inherit the challenge of getting enough qualified developers to follow these steps towards the Semantic Web closely. Trying to use automated scripts to generate the necessary identifiers for the Semantic Web will reduce the needed manpower to convert the data, but come with a rather high developing need during the starting phase.

3.3 Linking data
The major questions in linking data remain: What links are useful? When should be linked? Should every related kind of data be linked?

Those questions remain unanswered in detail. By now it is more of a question how much data one can link instead of which data one should link. As long as there are not too many links available it is still a good idea to link as much related data as possible to increase the value of the information through more context. The more data is linked, the more difficult it will become to judge which additional data will really add value to the data. Recent developments in the internet world have shown that it is not difficult to find additional data to one topic, but more of a task to find relevant data within the findings. The simple conclusion of this experience every user can relive is the necessity of additional rules or at least principles what should be linked.

---

8 http://www.w3.org/DesignIssues/LinkedData.html

9 http://linkeddata.jiscpress.org/

7

Firstly the data being linked should really add value to the information. To ensure this it shall include relevant and different parts. If there is already a link in place that adds the same information from an other source it shall be recognizable that the new link is simply an additional source. Secondly the new links shall be accessible in the same extent and not lead to pages that are known to be of doubtful availability. The third issue is the reliability of the linked data. Only data that is really found at reliable sources shall be linked. Even if the web community eliminates wrong links within short times, this is not always the case. The well know Kazakhstan issue on Wikipedia is enough evidence that this is not always the case.[10]

This shows that simply relying on the self-organization effects of the web to get data linked might not be enough. Especially data with scientific importance need to be watched by administrators, who keep track of the changes and the sense of links. On the other side even huge amounts of users cannot fulfill the task of creating all necessary links, so that more scientific projects will remain very important to establish guidelines, that are understandable enough to be widely followed.

On the other side Berners-Lee simply calls for some common sense considerations on what one will link[2]. Obviously this can work as long as open government data is mainly used by a professional public. In the long term there shall be some more rules needed, like e. g. Wikipedia introduced them after the experience with intentionally wrong entries meant as user jokes. Since the whole open linked data movement is rather young and especially governments around the world jumped on it rather late, the necessity of such rules will occur over time. Right now things are expressed in the forms of do's and don'ts[11] or a code of conduct like in Britain[12] rather than in rules. It might even be too early for such fixed rules yet.

From the current point of view the project leaders need more support in linking data, mainly searching for more reasonable links and desiring a positive evolution of quality.

3.4 Standards

Providing data and reusing it are rather different, since the data formats that have been in place for years usually need a lot of adjustment to be usable for the desired applications. Especially TXT and CSV formats always need to be imported and restructured to other standards, but there is also a lot of experience with them.

Now the main issue of standardization is the usage of Resource Description Framework (RDF) language[13]. Linked data principles are the main guideline that is being followed on the path to the semantic web. These standards are set by organizations that are non-governmental and therefore not binding, but still it is visible that they are widely followed to make the projects for Linked Open Government Data successful.

For the generations of RDF there have been tries to use simple scripts following the according ontologies. Those scripts shall be highly reusable. This creates the necessity for developers to briefly understand the data, so that they can anticipate how the scripts can be used for future data sets. In general this has been a hazard for the forthcoming of these projects. The delays mainly result from the time taken for the combination of the knowledge from different participating groups.

The main identifier needed is the RDF triple, which consists of:

---

10 Wikipedia had to deactivate the content to Kazakhstan after fans of the comedy movie "Borat" kept filling it with movie jokes instead of facts about the country. The self control of the web community failed in that case.

11 http://www.w3.org/DesignIssues/GovData.html

12 Http://data.gov.uk/faq.htm#q17

13 http://www.w3.org/RDF/

- URL – e .g. www.data.gov/folder0/dataset0
- Title – e. g. gross domestic product of year 19yy -20yy
- Publisher – e. g. Ministry of Finance coutry0

Such simple RDF triple can be created by running simple scripts based on existing or tailor-made ontologies[14] that are rather large and built to represent entire domains [1]. As soon as data should be of the highest possible quality, some work cannot be transferred to automatic scripts[15].

3.5 License
Thinking of licenses we must be aware that Open Data can be linked in several ways. By definition Open Data shall not be restricted in use. However, this is not true for all possible data that can be linked to it. At what extent can we link non-open data to open data? This is answered in rather different ways. For example the Europeana foundation states that no links shall be made to page that have some kind of commercial content, even including the BBC. [16]

Using this practice we get to a certain point of difficulty. As soon as data deals with business and infrastructural issues there might be the necessity to place links to some commercial or semi-commercial web pages in order to give enhanced value to the data. Refraining from this would leave useful resources unlinked and restrict the possibilities to increase data value.

On the side of commercial use there is often the problem of not completely free use and republishing. It can be rather difficult to be absolutely sure of the attached rights in foreign countries. The Open Knowledge Foundation has recently criticized this unclear situation. They focused on the unclear intellectual property rights of public bodies in several countries and collisions with database copyrights like recently decided in the Netherlands (see 5.3). The issue about it remains that in the European Union database rights automatically come into existence, while this is not the case in the USA.

Different copyright laws and the unresolved question about linking open and use-restricted data [4] provide several challenges for the further development towards more Semantic Web support.

3.6 Metadata
In addition to the data itself metadata is needed to describe the data. This machine readable metadata is one of the core elements for linking data towards the semantic web [2].

The metadata is the identifier for the data set that must follow some minimum requirements according to the DERI guide[17] of July 2010:
- published and maintained by a single provider

- available as RDF

- accessible, e. g. through dereferenceable HTTP URIs

Desired information within the metadata are:

– category of the data

---

14 e. g. http://www.geneontology.org/ http://sig.biostr.washington.edu/projects/fm/

15 compare chapter 5.1 and 5.2 for different practical approaches

16 http://www.europeana.eu/portal/

17 e. g. for the voID vocabulary for consumers and data providers: http://void-impl.googlecode.com/svn/trunk/guide/voiD-guide_v63.pdf

- title
- creator
- publisher
- date created and issued
- license type (open, copyright)
- technical description

Obviously the full amount of metadata would be the best to realize, but since workforce is always limited, it can be impossible to add everything. In certain projects described in chapter 5 decisions had to be made which way to follow, add more quality through metadata increase or open more data sets to linkage leading towards semantic web standards.

4. Semantic Web

More than simply linking data there have been efforts to create something more useable. After the steps of the Internet being mostly readable and becoming interactive having been named Web 2.0, lately there has been a development towards something that could be called Web 3.0. An essential part of this is the so called Semantic Web. In the Semantic Web the different places of data are no longer simply connected by links, but being connected in a more integral way. The information sources are linked so that the useful information is linked directly instead of a complete web page being linked. Technically Semantic Web Technology simply means that the links are performed in RDF language. Such links can be used by applications directly in much more divers ways than simple page links.

A Spanish project for Geographical Linked Data from the Polytechnic University of Madrid[18] uses Spreadsheets, Oracle and MySQL database sources connected to a web application. This project shows the possibilities of using existing ontologies even if they are in a different language than desired [8].

Ontologies are large complex data models that include information needed for such projects. From the economic point of view, it is not applicable for such rather small projects to build their own ontology to cover every aspect of the planned project. The nature of openness in the whole emerging Semantic Web environment gives the possibility to use an existing ontology or a network of existing ontologies.

Since the Semantic Web must rely on Linked Data as an essential component, Berners-Lee published his five star model for Open Linked Data in 2010:[19]

★ *Available on the web (whatever format), but with an open licence*

★★ *Available as machine-readable structured data (e.g. excel instead of image scan of a table)*

★★★ *as (2) plus non-proprietary format (e.g. CSV instead of excel)*

★★★★ *All the above plus, Use open standards from W3C (RDF and SPARQL) to identify things, so that people can point at your stuff*

★★★★★ *All the above, plus: Link your data to other people's data to provide context*

---

18 www.geolinkeddata.es

19 http://www.w3.org/DesignIssues/LinkedData.html

In addition to the listed above he introduced metadata as an additional requirement in 2010.

Finally the whole intention of the Semantic Web is to make data and information easily combine-able by automatic devices. This idea highlights the importance of the meta-data again, which is a necessary core element to be interpreted by automatic agents. One of the effects of the data being prepared for such automatic use and conversion will be a more graphical web in general. Of cause there is still a long way to go towards the so called Web 3.0 with Semantic Web reality in large scale. The year 2015 comes up as the time frame for this transition, given a similar developing speed that was taken towards Web 2.0 [3] [4] [7] [16].

5. International Use
Different approaches and different extends of data availability can be found all over the world.

5.1 United Kingdom
The British approach is focusing on simplicity. Data.gov.uk is built using open source and open standards to provide Open Data. Data sets are available for download as raw data in CSV, TXT, XML and Excel formats. There are some other formats like MSSQL, PDF and already some RDF linked data available. By the end of 2010 data.gov.uk still grows towards semantic web standards.

The British approach heavily invites the public to participate in the development. Using the workforce of the online community they try to get the project going much faster than simply relying on paid public servants. The strong advantage of a community-based participation is the possibility to break down complex problems to very small issues that can be solved by different co-producers individually until it is completely successful.

Still in the UK the focus is on high quality RDF data sets, even though the amount of those is still limited. Only selected data sets are made available this way, which is solely due to limited resources. Mostly the data is provided in raw data formats in the meantime. The promise to provide the data sets in machine readable formats has mainly been fulfilled with CSV files by the end of 2010. It appears like the British government is hoping that help from outside will set in and bring the desired resources for free and this seems to work rather well.

This has been called a "self-service approach" since it takes the consumer of the data some work, with just a standard RDF scheme and possibility to republish the data after connection and conversion of the data. In addition to this practice there is a standard scheme [4] the Digital Enterprise Research Institute (DERI) has developed. It is called 'dcat' and the further development will be performed by the eGovernment Interest Group of W3C. This scheme shall automatize generation of Unique Resource Identifiers (URI) from existing cell data of data provided in tables, e. g. CSV. The project shall even create RDF classes etc. to finally make it possible to link the data nearly automatically.

For targeting the published data right there was an online survey to gather information from a large number of people. The response ratio was rather limited with less than one hundred participants, over the time-frame of more than one month.

In addition to the national project, there have been several local and regional pages providing open data e. g. the city of London. All the British projects have bounded themselves to open data principles and open licenses. The UK government even announced the that they will make any raw data set available in the form of linked data.

11

During the process of publishing it seemed like opening government data and following linked data standards have become contrary targets. At least it was shown that strictly following these standards has become a hazard to opening the data rapidly. Clearly the British projects are much further in opening government data than in making them available according to semantic web principles. Anyway the continuous attempts to combines both successfully has clearly strengthened linked data standards.

5.2 USA

In the US the Open Data issue was started by the Open Government Directive from December 2009. The demand of "three high value datasets" to be published within 45 days after the directive by government agencies resulted in a rapid growth of available data within a few month. Once this process had been started the amount of available data sets grew much further than than the minimum demand by law. The encouragement for public participation has attracted third parties [5] to build tools and web applications around the data.

The impact of figures like stimulus money spending to certain areas has been tremendous. A huge amount of users have shown interest in the information sources linking this data to show where the money has gone, both regional and by industrial sectors.[20]

Amounts of more than 100 new published data sets per month have established during 2010. The voting system of zero to five stars gives the web community the possibility to rate the data. Somehow most votes are either zero or five stars.

In the USA several data sets are already converted to RDF data. The amount of these is not really an indication of the comparable progress towards semantic web. Since data.gov used rather simple algorithms to convert data towards RDF the quality is not comparable to the British practice. The rapid and less quality focused development in the USA is also connected to the Open Government Directive that uses rather pushy wordings to accelerate opening data. The side effect has been a focus on sheer amounts of data published.

The US government even promised to open all proposed legislation five days before signing, but still it is waited to become reality.

Even if not every target that was announced could be reached within the planned time, the new openness of US governmental data owners has found wide appreciation. These reactions and the need to prove the willingness of transparency will certainly encourage other countries to open their data.

5.3 Europe (EU)

In the EU there is not one single project uniting the data, but several national ones, even through knowledge transfer with unified standards within the EU would be desirable. Sweden, Denmark, The Netherlands, Austria and Spain have been the relatively early birds among the EU states. While Spanish data is widely available, it is mainly indirectly there through universities etc. The Scandinavians had a head-start in Europe. Austria is planning major efforts for 2011.

---

20 e.g. IT.USAspending.gov / recovery.gov

Sweden provides most data by now. The Swedish opengov.se provides just very little information in English, but a considerable amount of data sets in Swedish. The page is a private initiative just supported by public data and the provided data formats are rather simple. The semantic web ideas have not really been implemented by now. Even though RDF and XML data is announced, by now the main available formats are CSV, TXT and PDF. Norway and Denmark also started mainly with raw data, that is also available on pan-European basis.

The only pan-European project is Eurostat, uniting statistical data from EU and EFTA countries. The idea behind Eurostat is much older than open government and goes back to 1953[21]. It provides simply statistical data and does not follow semantic web rules by now. Even though the data is not linked in any way, the provided amount of data is enormous and has every possible chance to grow even bigger than the already well-linked British and American projects. Most of the data is as open for use and republishing as possible.

In Spain there is a remarkable development, that the regional government of Catalonia launched an open government portal[22] before the Spanish state did. Now that the Spanish state has gone live with its page, they cooperate with the in December 2010 launched Italian project http://www.datagov.it/. By now both projects remain in their local language. Mayor developments and opening of many data sets are announced for 2011. The Spanish government ranks itself as the top European country in e-participation, even before the UK and just behind Korea and Australia worldwide. According to their planning published in a strategy paper for the coming years [16] Spain doesn't want to drop back in comparison of online public service available. Within this plan the government understands its data sets as an economic factor of growth which they need to open, in order to support to increase international competitiveness.

In Germany such efforts are still not started. There has been a private initiative for more open government data in Germany.[23] It is planned for 2013 to publish open government data on a national basis in Germany. The decision for this project was taken on the nation IT convention an December 7th 2010 and no real steps could be taken in the meantime. Nevertheless regional public services have already started steps into the world of open data. Especially environmental data can already be accessed on open data basis and some even follows the principles of semantic web, e. g. water quality data for the river Rhine.[24] Still all those efforts are regional and not an a national basis by now.

Austria is planning to start its main efforts in 2011. By now the open government data is published on pages of private non-profit organizations. On the governmental page in Austria consists more of plans than data by the end of December 2010. The timetable for several conferences on the path to more open government data is already set and appears well planned, but comparably slow if we take the British approach as a reference.

France even tried to restrict access to existing web data and is trying to even restrict it more. There were efforts to make less data available to foreigners, even within the EU.

---

21 http://epp.eurostat.ec.europa.eu/portal/page/portal/eurostat/home/

22 http://www.proyectoaporta.es/web/guest/noticias_mes_12_10_aporta

23 http://opendata-network.org/

24 http://www.gov20.de/

The French stopped this restriction process on December 16th 2010 after international protest. It would have been doubtful that they could have really restricted access since the EU PSI Directive of 2003[25] lays down 'freedom of information' in general. In the Netherlands there has even been a court decision in 2009 limiting governmental ability to limit re-usage rights of the published data[26]. French courts would have been forced to decide similarly under the frame of European EU laws and contracts. Even though the legal base seems clear, it is sure that the French restriction efforts have slowed down the opening movement in Europe. It took massive protest from organizations like Regards Citoyens and Access Info Europe to stop the proposed law that would have been contrary to the opening of data in Europe.[27]

Some countries stepped forward to open up government data and see economical advantages in the new openness and transparency. The back-markers in this movement might face some critical voices that will result in economic disadvantages. The main issue in Europe will be the national ways and their differences. While Britain, Spain and the Scandinavian countries started serious efforts, they all chose on their own individual way. If one day a desire to harmonize all government data in Europe will come up, the differences being created in the actual phase of the projects will lead to new challenges and hazards asking to be overcome.

5.4 Australia and New Zealand
Australia has also started a project australia.gov.au which links the existing government data on several Australian pages and new published data sets. The project is in a rather early phase mainly linking existing pages with modern technologies. Some data sets are provided in formats[28] for geographical tools, that are not easily usable for the broad masses of web users. Other data that clearly aims at the man from the street e. g. a data set about barbecue places in the highly urbanized east coast area is provided in formats like Excel, CSV, XML or TXT.

Since the Australian page is still emerging and collecting data from different government agencies, they explicitly state the known existence of usability issues. It is obvious that the page is still in the development process and mainly connects what was already there. A lot of the provided data is rather old, even going back to 2003 as the latest data for certain categories.

A second Australian project is http://data.nsw.gov.au/ initiated by the region New South Wales. Some of the data is available in both, but there are nearly no similarities in appearance. However, both of the pages widely follow the rules of the semantic web.

---

25 Directive 2003/98/EC of the European Parliament and the Council of 17 November 2003

26 European Public sector Infromation Plattform:
   http://www.epsiplus.net/guest_blogs/open_government_data_in_the_netherlands

27 http://www.regardscitoyens.org/
   http://www.access-info.org/en/open-government-data

28 e. g. ESRI Grid format for the Forests of Australia 2003 including a clear mistake, publishing 2003 data under publishing date 1996-01-01

New Zealand's governmental page http://data.govt.nz/ is also in place for a comparably long time. It was started in November 2009 and clearly shows that it has come a much longer way than the Australian web offer. Several data sets are available in more than one data format. Even though some data is only linked in HTML at first, a PDF export is always available. It is clearly stated that this data is made available to promote economic growth. The New Zealand Government Technology Service is far enough, to ask the public for the data they desire to be made public in addition to what is already there. What is mainly different about their approach is the idea to have not only governmental publishers. New Zealand also invited owners of survey data and other relevant non-personal data to make their material available through their page. The upload link is already there on the starting page among the five major bullet points.

It appears like New Zealand has become the most advanced of the viewed open government web presences by now, even though their realization of semantic web principles have not proceeded as far as seen in other English speaking countries. The user friendlessness is also an issue. Scientists can find their desired data easily. If New Zealand is able to link the data according to semantic web rules they will become a reference projects for the followers that will enter the world of linked open government data.

6. Using the data
The provided data can be used in different ways. The traditional use was simply to download the data sets and import them to local applications. This will remain suitable for many highly specialized purposes in future. Through the emerging of semantic web technology the weight of web applications has increased and will continue this path. The third important development has been web visualization tools that make it rather easy to understand complex data even for people just becoming interested due to its new easiness. Especially the public interest in the USA [5] has shown how much easy access attracts views and even participation.

6.1 Download and Local Applications
The classic government data to be found on the web was mainly there in very small and size-efficient formats like CSV and TXT. This used to be the best way to transfer data in the past, where size did matter a lot for the time needed. Especially large data amounts took very long to be downloaded and compatibility was a much larger issue than today.

Some data today is still best to be provided in such formats in order to be useable to several applications. Data imports to table formats like Excel or database formats are rather easy. On the other hand those formats offer very little options. Modern applications supporting many modern formats are available as open source. In this environment it becomes more common to provide data in database formats together with links to the according free software [10].

The clear advantage of these traditional formats is, that the existing data is simply opened to the public and like in the British approach the task to link it is left to the participants that put their efforts into it on a non-paid bases. The cost attached to this path is relatively low for the governmental agencies and a visible success can be shown within very short time.

6.2 Web Applications

The development and availability of fast web technology to most people in developed countries has provided an opportunity for web based technologies and applications. One advantage of web based applications is clearly the fact that no installation to a local computer is needed, a normal web browser is usually enough.

An application with rather obvious advantages of the web based approach is earthquake data combination and visualization[29]. Data can be added in real time from around the world [10] and every user online can provide some temporary computer resource for the application's calculation while watching the data. The web based applications in general make the user more independent of the individual end user device power, e. g. the recently popular tablet PCs or Smart-phones cannot provide the same power for the necessary calculation to visualize information on large scale maps which are among the most popular web based application use on a mobile end user devices.

There are also possibilities for nearly every user to build their own applications. Several tool-kits are available to click together tools for special pages. In March 2010 the New York Times entered the stage in this field, they offer a ready "Who Went Where" application to enable finding former schoolmates within the USA. On top of this they not only provide the source code, but also a very small course to building the reader's own application.[30]

The development towards more web based applications is also connected with the whole cloud computing issue being largely pushed forward by companies like Microsoft and Yahoo. There can be applications like previously known to be held local e. g. office tools and database querying. While tables have always been a very common form for queried data to be presented, there are many more possibilities nowadays. The most important form of web based applications results in visualization applications that combine database queries with a graphical component. Obvious advantages of such a presentation is the useability on small screens like mobile phones.

6.3 Visualization

On top of the possibilities of web based solutions there are also ready to access visualizations. Such visualizations have web applications in behind, that are more or less noticed by the users. Especially geographical data that is linked with other data can be much easier to consume for more people once it is applied on maps.

The Spanish geolinkeddata.es combines most recent semantic web technology [8] with a very familiar view for many users. It appears like a long known route planning or localization tool. The initiators of the project use a Google Maps interface together with the open technology that Google provides.

---

29 e. g. http://data-gov.tw.rpi.edu/wiki/Demo

30 http://open.blogs.nytimes.com/2010/03/30/build-your-own-nyt-linked-data-application/

An other linked Geo-data source that can be used for visualization purposes is the OpenStreetMap project[31]. Since the visualizations with maps are very popular, statistical data is applied to maps has become popular among developers, too. One project combining these in a rather simple way was called "How good is my area?"[32] combining statistical data like crime, health, income, education and employment rates with a map view to show "quality of areas". Such an application might really be used in the U.K. e. g. by buyers for houses. Of cause this application was only an example applications from the University of Southampton to show what could easily be developed. Their EnAKTing project is aiming to create useful visualizations that are simple to create. Everything is based on data.gov.uk until the end of 2010 with still many room to start further visualization applications on the growing data amounts.

One major future development to be expected in visualizations can be report generating software like Infomaker and Crystal Reports. Since such software products even give not highly trained users the chance to generate results from databases, they provide many opportunities for republished data from private sides and initiatives working on non-profit bases. Open source movement has always adopted existing useful tools for the use of a wide range of online community members. There is an emerging need for more such software under open source standards for easy and fast to build visualizations.

7. Target Group of Government Data

All the preparations for better usage and effectiveness of the data add possibilities and value to the data sets. Anyway the real value of the data sets is not measurable on a collective basis. What might be perfect for governmental organizations could be more of a hazard for scientific or business use. Therefore it needs to be considered who is going to use the data. In marketing such is done by a target group analysis. Since open government data sets are finally financed by the taxpayer the extend of such tasks is limited in order not to waste money. On the other hand the economic value added through useful data can be enormous.

Open data provided by governmental organizations can be used in business for several purposes. Business development always relies on data sources that are external to a company. The providers of such data can also have commercial interest in the decisions, which results in a collision of interests. Open data on the other hand will be rated by the enormous masses of web users that in the end seem rather similar to the target group of many commercial activities. Small businesses that wouldn't be able to buy much information from different sources. The availability of open data sources gives them a rather fair chance compared to the information advantage the big players had in the past. Of cause the idea that open data will help to increase competitiveness of small and midsize companies is limited, but anyway it can be a small step towards a widely desired functioning of markets and competition.

Local authorities will find ways to highlight the advantages of their areas for prospective investors. On this side of the interested parties there might arise strong efforts to use such data to attract companies. The sheer amount of web users and other competing local authorities will ensure a certain equality of competition within the semantic web. The visibility of advantages of more rural areas can definitely increase through a well planned connection and fitting links on the semantic web.

---

31 http://openstreetmap.org

32 http://myarea.psi.enakting.org/

Scientists have a much clearer view on what data they need and for which purposes. For science the data can hardly be enough to get good results. There is no interest in simple strengths and weaknesses of areas and data useless for business users might add some information content. Therefore it is important not to leave the Government Data Sets within the semantic web to the business side of the web. Scientists around the world will widely benefit from open data, which will finally result in a gain of information and knowledge to the whole society.

Non-profit-organizations that must always keep track of their costs very carefully to fulfill their purpose can also get better data without much cost attached. In the past missing data could lead to wrong conclusions and efforts on the wrong side of an issue. Openly available data sources will help them to judge on the necessity of projects in different areas. For example there might be a lack of education in some areas of a country. If one connects data of schools with data of population density the information value increases. By linking this data to roads, bus routes and railways towards the towns with schools the data increases further. Such data is generally owned by governments of these countries, the availability to the groups that need the data has not always been granted in the past.

The one target group never really mentioned in the discussion about Open Government data is the press. This group is rather special for the data publishers since they might not really be interested in the data itself, but in the message given by opening the data. Opening data like stimulus and recovery money for certain industrial sectors or regions shows a certain amount of transparency. On the other hand, opening the data at the wrong time might cause side-effects that are not desired, e. g. similar economic help in competing countries or areas. This provides conflicting aims in opening data sets as well. Transparency is clearly a driving force behind opening government data, but there might be fears that this increasing transparency might hurt valuable other aims, like recently in France. For the journalists such thoughts can easily appear like a path to less transparency and simply give a different impression than the idea behind.

These and possible other groups of users should always be kept in mind when decisions of publishing or linkage are made. Different target groups will emerge and develop over time which makes the considerations of 'who will use the data' need to be repeated over time to match the changing need of a unknown future.

8. OUTLOOK

Naturally governments don't want to increase the competitiveness of foreign companies paying their taxes elsewhere, but point out the advantages of their national economy. As long as the decision makers think publishing open data supporting their aims, this process will increase.

The contrary development within the European Union has shown that the new openness with government data is widely appreciated. Restriction efforts result in confrontations that either end in court decisions or a form of surrender or those who wanted to restrict the availability of open data. Most countries start web services for open data, either in old fashioned web technologies or even try to establish linked data already.

The amount of data has always increased since the early days of computers entering the worlds of business and public service. The technical development has supported and will go on to support more and more data to be collected and used. These amounts of data might be useful or useless, sometimes only depending on the contexts they can be used. Since this has been widely understood during the last few years, linked data is now the center of attention. The realization of these links is becoming more and more user friendly through the semantic web.

The way towards data sets being published with meta-data in RDF or similar standards will continue. There is still a giant amount of data already published that is lacking meta-data. The workload to add such meta-data can hardly be over-estimated and might be impossible for governments to include everything.

Like already done in the UK the call for help towards the community to join forces to turn data into linked data is to be expected in many more countries. The ones entering the stage rather late might have an advantage in understanding of the technologies from the beginning of their projects, but still the enthusiasm of helping hands from the online community might be reduced a lot once these technologies start to lack the attractive 'glamorously new' look of something really new. Countries like Germany that want to start rather late might face disadvantages in science and even economics from not being able to show advantages through open data.

Through the mega-trend towards mobile technologies the visualizations mostly used will surely become map applications linked with semantic web data. Such applications will include popular leisure time applications like water quality checks on a beach to business and scientific applications, e. g. for infrastructure that certain areas provide for prospective investors.

Governmental data will also attract a completely new group of viewers being simply politically interested and trying to find out what is happening why. The US effort have shown that there is a growing interest in regional data. Projects like the new tunnel through the Gotthard mountains in Switzerland or "Stuttgart 21" attract much attention to their web presented data, one because people are fascinated, the other because they want to plan protests against. Over all, both are sides of the same thing, growing interest in governmental projects and more transparency. From the view of showing willingness towards more transparency opening governmental data sets has become a powerful instrument. This shall lead to more open government data on the web, since this gives politicians the chance to appear in favorable ways and proving transparency efforts.

In the industrialized countries such open data sets provided by governments can also be used to show comparative advantages over low-wage countries, where they are.

9. CONCLUSION

The path from simply opening data to open linked data has been started. It appears like an irreversible movement that has been started. Even the international crisis on the financial markets might help the open data movement, since the calls for more transparency got louder along with every new discovery of hidden bad practice.

The US and the UK have started to establish large amounts of open government data and link it in to Linked Open Government Data (LOGD), closely followed by the Scandinavian countries and Spain. Even though Germany and France are big players that have not joined into this trend, the sheer number of countries moving the same way will make them follow, too. It can also be seen as a rather conservative view related to new technologies in these two big European countries, who usually used to be rather among the second group to join such tends in the past as well.

The linked data principles provide many new opportunities for data usage. Getting all the existing data connected under the rules for semantic web will take several years if ever really completed. Still there is the chance for semi-automatic transformation like already practiced in the US, but with considerable lower quality compared to the mainly manual curated British approach. In the end a mixture of both might be the only way, since many data sets might not be worth the the manual work and automatic transformation by multiple-use scripts is the efficient way.

More web based applications are going to appear in future, since major players in the software industry push towards the so called cloud computing. On the open source side the possibilities seem endless in the world of the semantic web. Most standards and applications for the semantic web are connected with the open source movement, either through people supporting both or one standard emerging form one to the other movement.

Still the availability of the data sets in old fashioned formats like CSV and TXT remain very useful for importing data to different programs. Especially in the world of science and education there can be rather simple tools being more powerful for a certain purpose than commercial complex software. Since governments have a special interest in these areas it can be expected that even linked open government data will remain available in simple formats for download.

These formats will be surviving the implementation of semantic web technology. Even today governmental web pages provide data in several formats. The ever growing amount and power of the available technology will make such practice consistently easier over time.

In 2011 we stand the beginning of the development Governmental Data will take into the world of Open Linked Data and the Semantic Web.

10. REFERENCES

[1] Alani, Harith and others, Unlocking the potential of public sector information with semantic web technology, The Open University, U.K. 2007

[2] Berners-Lee, Tim, Linked Data, Website: http://www.w3.org/DesignIssues/LinkedData.html 2006-07-27, (Update 2009/06/18)

[3] Berners-Lee, Tim, Putting Government Data online, June 2009

[4] Campbell, L. M. and MacNeill, S., The Semantic Web, Linked and Open Data, JISC cetis, U.K. June 2010

[5] Castro, D., What's Next for Open Government?, USA, March 3rd 2010

[6] Cyganiak, Richard and others, Self-Service Linked Government Data with dcat and Gridworks, Graz / Austria, September 2010

[7] Davies, Tim, Open data, democracy and public sector reform, MSc Dissertation at University of Oxford, U.K. August 2010

[8] de León, A. and others, Geographical Linked Data: a Spanish Use Case, Spain 2010

[9] Ding, Li, and others, Making Sense of Open Government Data, Renselaer Polytechnic Institute USA 2010

[10] Ding, Li and others, The Data-gov Wiki: A Semantic Web Portal for Linked Government Data, USA 2009

[11] Ding. Li amd others, TWC Data-Gov Corpus: Incrementally Generating Linked Government Data from Data.gov, USA 2010

[12] DiFranzo, D. and others, TWC LOGD: A Portal for Linking Open Government Data, Rensselaer Polytechnic Institute USA 2010

[13] Herzig, Daniel, Linked Data – Grundlagen Einführung ins Data Web, Karlsruhe Institut of Technology, 2010

[14] Sheridan, J and Tennison, J., Linking U.K. Government Data, U.K. April 2007

[15] Omitola. Tope and others, Put in your postcode, out comes the data: A case study, University of Southampton, March 2010

[16] unknown authors for the Ministerio De Industria, Turismo Y Comercio, Estrategia 2011 – 2015, plan Avanza 2, Madrid, July 16th 2010

[17] Watson, Mark, Practical Semantic Web and Linked Data Applications, USA 2010